DATE DUE

SEP 25 1991			

Facing the Future

RENEWABLE ENERGY

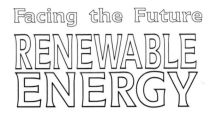

Facing the Future
RENEWABLE ENERGY

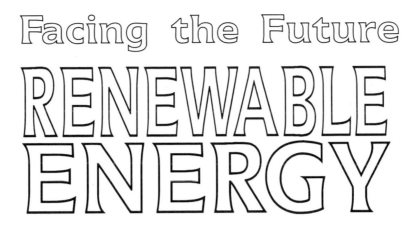

Alan Collinson

STECK-VAUGHN
LIBRARY
A Division of Steck-Vaughn Company
Austin, Texas

Published in the United States in 1991
by Steck-Vaughn Company, Austin, Texas

Library of Congress Cataloging-in-Publication Data

Collinson, Alan.
  Renewable energy / Alan Collinson.
    p. cm. — (Facing the future)
  Includes index.
  Summary: Discusses possible renewable energy resources for the future, such as solar power, wind farms, the energy of moving water, and recycling.
    ISBN 0-8114-2802-8
    1. Renewable energy sources—Juvenile literature.   [1. Renewable energy sources.]   I. Title.   II. Series.
  TJ808.2.C65   1991
  333.79′4—dc20   90-19791
                                                      CIP AC

Typeset by David Seham Associates, Metuchen, NJ
Printed in Hong Kong.
Bound in the United States by Lake Book, Melrose Park, IL
  2 3 4 5 6 7 8 9 0 HK 95 94 93 92

Acknowledgments

Maps and diagrams – Jillian Luff of Bitmap Graphics
Illustrations – Outline Illustration, Derby – Andrew Calvert, Andrew Cook, Andrew Staples
Design – Neil Sayer
Editor – Su Swallow

For their help and for information given the author and publishers wish to thank the following:

Club Med, Lloyd's Register of Shipping, the Japanese Merchant Shipping Agency, London.

For permission to reproduce copyright material the author and publishers gratefully acknowledge the following:

Cover photograph – The movable heat receiver at Texas Tech's Crosbyton solar power project aligns itself with the reflected sunlight. – U.S. Department of Energy.

Title page – Solar panel heating systems for heating water, Alanya, Turkey – Sheila Terry, Science Photo Library.

Page 7 – Alan Collinson; page 8 – Sekal, Zefa; page 9 – C.c. Lim, John Topham Picture Library; page 10 – E. Landschak, Zefa; page 11 – (top) Lynn Baker, Compix – (bottom) Peter Ryan, Science Photo Library; page 12 – Zefa; page 13 – Peter Menzel, Science Photo Library; page 14 – Robert Harding Picture Library; page 15 – Dr Peter Thiele, Zefa; page 16 – Andrew Hill, Hutchison Library; page 17 – (left) Trygve Bolstad, Panos Pictures – (right) Mark Boulton, ICCE;

page 18 – (top) Hutchison Library – (middle) David Lomax, Robert Harding Picture Library – (bottom) Sullivan and Rogers, Bruce Coleman Limited; page 20 – (top) Molyneux Photography – (bottom) "Club Med T – Club Med's Sailing Cruiser"; page 21 – Peter Menzel, Science Photo Library – (inset) Ken Lucas, Planet Earth Pictures; page 22 – (top left) Bramaz, Zefa – (bottom left and center) Martin Bond, Science Photo Library – (bottom right) John Lythgoe, Planet Earth Pictures; page 23 – Voigtmann, Zefa; page 24 – (top and bottom) Martin Bond, Science Photo Library; page 25 – Martin Bond, Science Photo Library; page 26 – J. Pfaff, Zefa; page 27 – Robert Harding Picture Library; page 28 – (top) Alan Collinson – (bottom) Martin Bond, Science Photo Library; page 29 – Jonathan Wright, Bruce Coleman Limited – (inset) Images Colour Library; page 30 – Intermediate Technology; page 33 – (left) Handford Croydon, Zefa – (middle) Robert Harding Picture Library – (right) Walter Rawlings, Robert Harding Picture Library; page 34 – (top) George Hulton, Science Photo Library – (bottom) Simon Fraser, Science Photo Library; page 35 – Alan Collinson; page 36 – Alan Collinson; page 37 – (top) © Dwight Ellefsen/Shostal/Superstock – (bottom) Sally Margan, Ecoscene; page 38 – The ECD Partnership (main picture: the Hughes Home, Milton Keynes); page 39 – (top left) Creda Ltd – (top right) Philips Lighting Ltd – (middle left) Juliet Highet, Hutchison Library – (middle and middle right) Rockwool Ltd – (bottom) The ECD Partnership; page 40 – (top) General Motors – (bottom) Paul Shambroom, Science Photo Library; page 41 – Jerry Mason, Science Photo Library; page 42 – Chris Howes, Planet Earth Pictures; page 43 – (left and right) Sue Cunningham, David Austen, Tony Stone Worldwide.

Contents

Introduction

The **fuels** we use now to give us heat, light, and power are being steadily used up. The main fuels are coal, oil, gas, and uranium. All of them are taken from rocks in the Earth's crust. Coal, oil, and gas were formed from the remains of plants and animals that died and became trapped in the rocks, so they are called **fossil fuels.** There is only a limited amount of each kind of fossil fuel. Once these fuels have been removed by mining, and consumed in power stations and factories, the **energy** they contain is gone forever. Not only are the fuels we use now limited in amount, they also pollute the air as we burn them. One of the fuels—uranium—leaves deadly wastes behind, as well.

The difficulties with these fuels will increase as the population of the world grows. At present there are just over 5 billion people in the world. By the year 2020 there will be over 7 billion people. If all these additional people use the same kinds and amounts of energy we use now, the fuels will be used up even faster than at present and the air will become even more polluted. This will have very serious results for all the world's peoples. For example, many scientists think that the extra gases we are adding by burning these fuels will change the world's climate and make it heat up. Deserts will grow and sea levels rise as the ice caps melt.

To avoid serious consequences of this kind, scientists, engineers, and others are searching for ways of harnessing other sources of energy such as sunlight and saltwater. These sources can provide power without pollution and will never be used up. They are **renewable energy sources.**

The chart opposite sets out the main renewable energy sources. They are already being used in many parts of the world, even though you may have few in your own area. Over the next few decades their use will become quite common. There are five main kinds: gravity, sunlight, recycled energy, the saltiness of seawater, and heat inside the Earth. The first three are closely linked. For example, the sun's heat evaporates the water from the sea. When this falls as rain and runs down river valleys, gravity makes the water move. We can build a dam to trap the moving water's energy and run the water through a hydroelectric power station, or use it more directly, to turn a waterwheel.

All five sources of energy are widely available. Why, then, have they not been used more in the past, to avoid the problems we now have with fossil fuels and uranium? The answer is that the energy in the fossil fuels and uranium is in a very concentrated form. Renewable energy sources, on the other hand, are very dilute (spread out). This makes them much more difficult to use than coal, oil, gas, or uranium. For example, when we burn coal it gives out twice as much heat as the same amount of wood. Oil gives out three times as much, and uranium thousands of times as much. The sun pours down vast amounts of energy, much more than we use from all the fossil fuels put together, but it is spread all over the planet.

In the last 100 years, engineers and scientists have learned how to extract the energy from fossil fuels and uranium. In the next 100 years they will have to devise ways to extract the energy from renewable energy sources. This book explores some of the ways already in use. Perhaps you are one of our future scientists or engineers who will continue the work on these sources. If not, you will certainly be somebody who uses energy produced from them.

fuels – any substances that provide energy to make things work.
fossil fuels – coal, oil, and natural gas (methane) obtained from plant and animal remains trapped in rocks. There are only limited amounts of these fuels left.
energy – something that is capable of making things work.
renewable energy sources – sources of energy that will not run out, no matter how much is used.

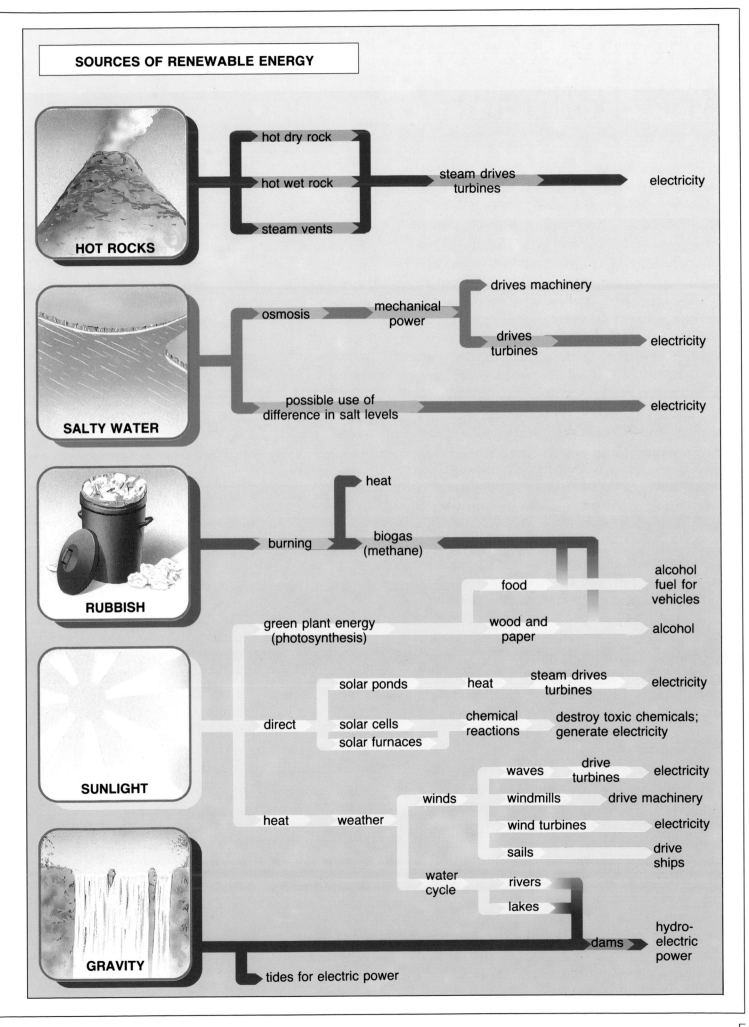

SOURCES OF RENEWABLE ENERGY

HOT ROCKS
- hot dry rock
- hot wet rock
- steam vents
→ steam drives turbines → electricity

SALTY WATER
- osmosis → mechanical power → drives machinery
- drives turbines → electricity
- possible use of difference in salt levels → electricity

RUBBISH
- burning → heat
- biogas (methane)

green plant energy (photosynthesis) → food → alcohol fuel for vehicles
- wood and paper → alcohol

SUNLIGHT
- direct
  - solar ponds → heat → steam drives turbines → electricity
  - solar cells / solar furnaces → chemical reactions → destroy toxic chemicals; generate electricity
- heat → weather
  - winds
    - waves → drive turbines → electricity
    - windmills → drive machinery
    - wind turbines → electricity
    - sails → drive ships
  - water cycle
    - rivers
    - lakes

GRAVITY
- dams → hydro-electric power
- tides for electric power

Energy, Poverty, and Pollution

Until about 250 years ago, people used very little energy. Most of the energy they needed came from renewable sources such as wind to drive windmills and sailing ships, water to drive waterwheels, and wood for cooking and for making pottery, glass, and metals. Then people found out how to use heat from wood—and then coal—to drive steam engines. About 100 years ago engineers invented the steam turbine (a large fan turned by a jet of steam) to drive electric generators. Once electricity could be produced in great quantities using the turbine, it could be sent almost anywhere by cables.

All these changes over the last 250 years are known as the Industrial Revolution. This revolution has led to the high standards of living we now have in the world's industrialized countries. These countries now need vast quantities of energy to keep their factories, offices, shops, homes, and transportation systems working. There are many other parts of the world that the Industrial Revolution has not touched. In most of Africa, South and Central America (named Latin America), India, China, and Southeast Asia a great majority of people still make their living from farming. Most of the world's 5 billion people live in these lands and are poor.

Rich and poor

One of the major differences between the richer and poorer countries is how much energy they use. The rich countries use 80 percent of the world's energy. Most of the poor countries want to catch up with the rich countries, but this is not easy. Even if they have coal or oil to use for industry, they have to borrow large amounts of money to build power stations and to buy machinery and technical advice. Paying back these loans can cripple the economy of poor countries even further. One way the poor countries could get richer is to use renewable energy sources.

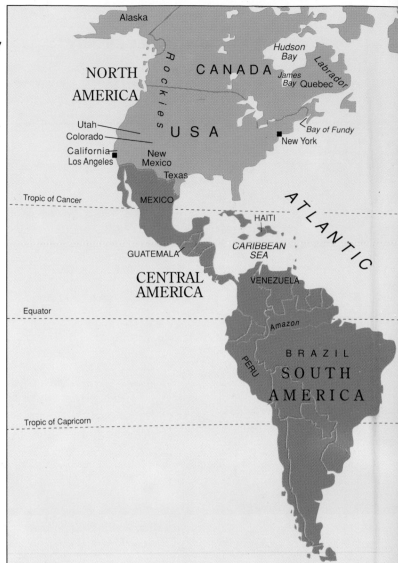

Most of the programs to produce power from renewable sources in poor countries have so far concentrated on building dams for hydroelectric power (see page 28). Building big dams is one of the most expensive ways of using renewable energy, and although the dams provide lots of electricity, they may not make enough money to pay back big loans. Other sources of renewable energy, such as the sun or wind or tides, could be much cheaper to use.

As we learn more about the best way to harness the forces of nature to provide our energy needs, the poor countries will adopt more and more of these techniques. The energy supply from renewable sources will then become even cheaper. It may be that in 20 or 30 years' time, some of the world's poorest countries will be using their abundant sunshine to generate some of the world's cheapest electricity.

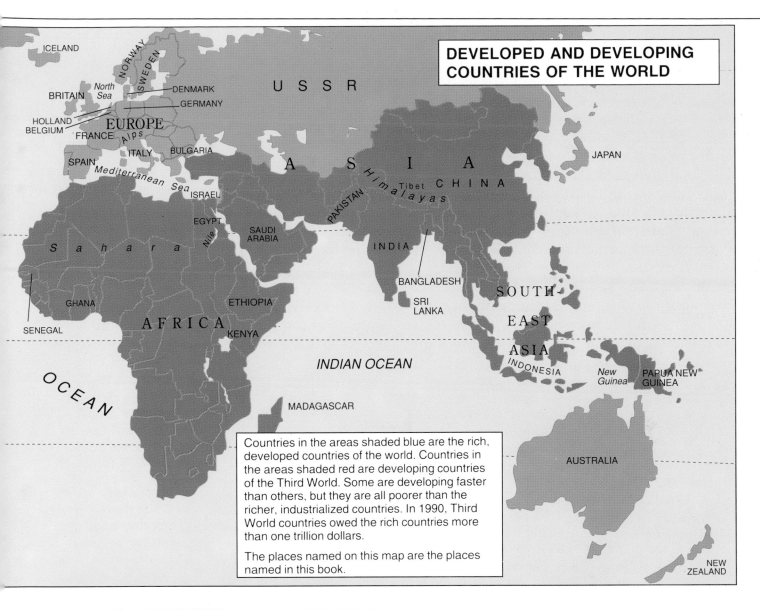

DEVELOPED AND DEVELOPING COUNTRIES OF THE WORLD

ICELAND
NORWAY
SWEDEN
BRITAIN
North Sea
DENMARK
GERMANY
HOLLAND
BELGIUM
EUROPE
FRANCE
Alps
SPAIN
ITALY
BULGARIA
Mediterranean Sea
ISRAEL
USSR
ASIA
Himalayas
Tibet
CHINA
JAPAN
PAKISTAN
EGYPT
Nile
SAUDI ARABIA
INDIA
BANGLADESH
Sahara
GHANA
ETHIOPIA
AFRICA
KENYA
SENEGAL
SRI LANKA
SOUTH-EAST ASIA
INDONESIA
New Guinea
PAPUA NEW GUINEA
OCEAN
INDIAN OCEAN
MADAGASCAR
AUSTRALIA
NEW ZEALAND

Countries in the areas shaded blue are the rich, developed countries of the world. Countries in the areas shaded red are developing countries of the Third World. Some are developing faster than others, but they are all poorer than the richer, industrialized countries. In 1990, Third World countries owed the rich countries more than one trillion dollars.

The places named on this map are the places named in this book.

Dumping coal waste in Durham, England. Fossil fuels cause pollution on the ground as well as in the air (see page 8). Here, a conveyor dumps coal waste from a mine onto the beach. Bulldozers push the waste into the North Sea. The waste is swept along the coast by the waves, and has killed off all the seashore life for almost 20 miles. Before the dumping began, this was one of the most beautiful coasts in Britain.

Energy and pollution

Burning lots of coal, oil, and gas pollutes the air. These fuels contain a chemical called carbon. When the fuels are burned the carbon joins with another chemical in the air, oxygen, to form carbon dioxide. As a result, the amount of carbon dioxide in the Earth's air as a whole is increased. This affects the temperature of the Earth's atmosphere. When the Earth is heated up by sunlight, some of the heat is absorbed by the carbon dioxide in the air. So the more carbon dioxide the air contains, the warmer it gets. The carbon dioxide acts like glass in a greenhouse. It lets in the light but does not let the heat back out. For this reason it is known as a **greenhouse gas.** It is believed that if the heating up of the air continues, very serious effects will follow. For instance, large amounts of the ice in Antarctica and the Arctic, and the world's mountains will melt. Countries such as Bangladesh, Holland, and even parts of the U.S. and Britain will be in danger of flooding. Deserts may get larger and areas such as the interiors of the U.S. and the Soviet Union will have severe droughts.

Most air pollution is caused by the industrialized countries. Some governments have already agreed to reduce the burning of fossil fuels in order to reduce the amount of greenhouse gases in the air. So poor countries are not likely to build many coal or oil power stations in the future, even if they could afford to. Cost and the greenhouse effect will

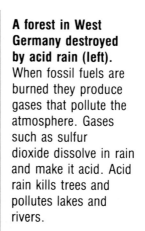

A forest in West Germany destroyed by acid rain (left). When fossil fuels are burned they produce gases that pollute the atmosphere. Gases such as sulfur dioxide dissolve in rain and make it acid. Acid rain kills trees and pollutes lakes and rivers.

No smoke without pollution (right). Smoke from the chimneys at power stations fills the air with gases that pollute the atmosphere.

Measuring Energy

To measure energy and work, a unit named the joule (pronounced *jool*) is used. Power, which is the rate of doing work, is measured in another unit named the watt. Both units are very small. For example, a 100 watt lamp uses 100 joules of energy in one second. These names and symbols are used for large numbers of units:

1,000 watts = 1 kilowatt (1 kw)
1,000,000 watts = 1 megawatt (1 MW)
1,000,000,000 = gigawatt (1 GW) or one billion watts
1,000,000,000,000 = 1 terrawatt (1 TW) or one trillion watts.

The word *watt* and the letter *W* can be replaced with the *joule* and the letter *J* in this list to give energy quantities.

When electrical power is bought and sold it is measured in the number of hours it is used. For example, one bar of an electric heater will use one kilowatt in one hour, so the cost would be for 1 kilowatt hour (1 kwh). To help you measure figures in this book you may like to remember that a large, modern coal-burning power station has a power output of about 2,000 megawatts (2,000 MW), and one megawatt is equivalent to one thousand 1 kw electric heaters.

force many poor countries into developing power supplies from renewable sources if they want to become richer. In the rich countries it will be the greenhouse effect that forces them to adopt renewable energy. Already many of the rich countries have begun to plan for this change. By the end of the century Denmark will be producing 10 percent of its electricity from the wind. Holland will be producing about five percent and Germany about two percent. As more is found out about the greenhouse effect, such figures for renewable energy will be common to many countries, rich and poor alike.

See for Yourself
● Each piece of electrical equipment in your home should have a label to tell you how much power, in watts, it needs to work. Add up all these figures (don't forget the electric lights) to find how much electrical power your home needs if all the devices were switched on. Everybody in a school class could do the same to get an average figure per household. Multiply this by the number of homes in your district.

greenhouse gases – gases that trap heat in the atmosphere. They include carbon dioxide, carbon monoxide, nitrous oxide (from car fumes and fertilizers), methane (from animal dung, oil and gas wells, peat, and rotting plants), and chemicals called CFCs (chlorofluorocarbons) from aerosols and refrigerator cooling liquid.

The Energy of the Sun

The Earth absorbs sunlight in two main ways. By far the greater amount goes to heating up the surface of the land and the sea. This heats the air and gives us our different kinds of weather. Without the heat in the air the Earth would have an average temperature of only 30°F (−1°C). In fact, its overall temperature is 59°F (15°C). It is this warmth that allows life to exist. People have been using the sun's free heat for thousands of years. Even when our ancestors lived in caves, they chose caves facing the sun. If you look at the map on page 6 and compare it with the one on this page you will see that many poor countries have lots of energy pouring down on them every day from the sun. This is very fortunate for them because they do not have to spend much on heating their homes, which would make them even poorer.

Light and life

The second way sunlight is absorbed at the Earth's surface is by green plants. Green plants contain a chemical called chlorophyll. Chlorophyll absorbs most of the white light that falls on it, but not the green light. This is reflected, which is why green plants are green. The light energy which is absorbed is used inside the leaves to make food chemicals. The whole process is called **photosynthesis**.

Growing crops in the sun. Steep cliffs facing south make an ideal site for these greenhouses in northern Italy. The glass allows sunlight to enter but then traps the heat, which helps the crops to grow.

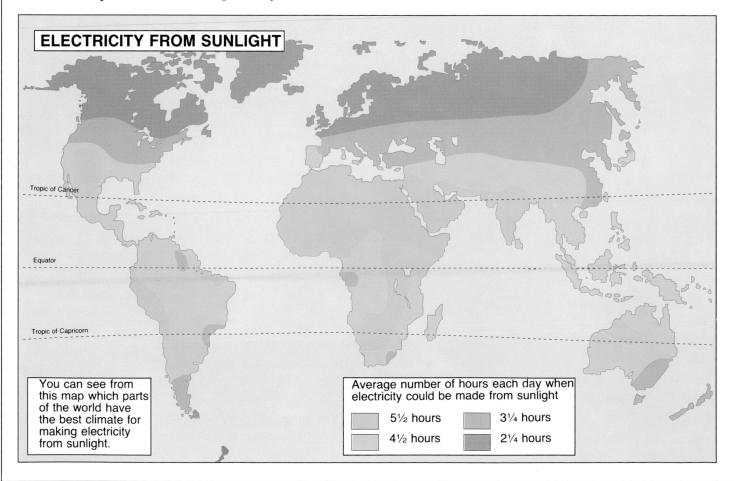

ELECTRICITY FROM SUNLIGHT

Tropic of Cancer

Equator

Tropic of Capricorn

You can see from this map which parts of the world have the best climate for making electricity from sunlight.

Average number of hours each day when electricity could be made from sunlight

5½ hours	3¼ hours
4½ hours	2¼ hours

All forms of life (except some very simple kinds) are dependent on photosynthesis for their food. Even animals that only eat meat are eating other animals which depend on green plants. In addition, about half the people of the world depend on photosynthesis for their supplies of fuel, in the form of wood. Wood is one of the substances plants make from their own food.

Even when we burn fossil fuels we are using a form of solar energy. In the distant past, the energy-containing chemicals which made up the bodies of plants and animals often became concentrated in sands and mud. Over a long time they changed to coal (layers of fossil wood) or oil, or they rotted and gave off natural gas. These fuels are therefore a fossilized form of solar energy.

Reflected sunlight

At a simple level, sunlight can be reflected into a container for cooking. Many solar stoves are used in poor countries now. In India, most stoves are solar-powered.

Sunlight can be used to drive machines. The sunlight is concentrated using many mirrors.

These mirror concentrators are expensive but they produce very high temperatures. The reflected light is focused onto a solar furnace. A liquid—usually an oil capable of absorbing large amounts of heat—is passed through the furnace and heated to high temperatures. The latest furnaces in California heat the oil to 748°F (398°C). This heat is then used to boil water, while the steam drives turbines to make electricity.

A solar-powered stove (above). Such utensils can be used for cooking a variety of food.

Putting the kettle on, in a village in Tibet (left). In poor countries solar power is being used more and more for heating water and for cooking.

The most frequent use of solar furnaces is to purify drinking water. They are particularly useful in hot, dry areas near the sea, or where the water from underground is not pure. The impure water from the sea, the underground, or from salty lakes is boiled using the solar furnace. When it turns to steam, the salts and impurities are left behind. When it cools, it condenses to purified water. The process is called **desalination** (salt removal). Often the salts can be sold, which reduces the cost of purifying. The U.S., Israel, Saudi Arabia, the Soviet Union, Bulgaria, and Australia all have solar desalination plants. By the year 2000, there will be many more of these plants, especially in poor, sunny countries with a long dry season. Even developed countries like France and Spain are planning solar desalination plants as industry's demands for water increase and supplies from rivers are no longer adequate.

Hotter than the sun

In spite of the many mirrors at a large solar power plant, only a small amount of the sun's energy is used. Engineers have always said that if they could reach greater light intensities, direct solar energy would become one of the world's major power sources. In 1989, this goal was achieved by scientists and engineers at the University of Colorado. The tube-shaped device they made is quite simple, but large-scale versions may be able to reach light intensities near (*or even beyond*) those of the sun's surface. This new solar concentrator could produce large amounts of cheap power, create brand new materials, and might also be used to destroy toxic (poisonous) chemicals. By 2010, this device may be the most common source of energy in sunny countries, rich and poor alike. This solar concentrator has been named the Winston tube, after the scientist who invented it.

Taking out the salt. The Dead Sea in Israel has the saltiest water in the world, but it can be purified for drinking. The water is heated by the sun in shallow ponds (inset). The heated water from the bottom of the pond is drawn off and it then turns to steam, leaving the salt behind. When the steam condenses back to water it can be used for drinking. The steam is also used to drive turbines to generate electricity.

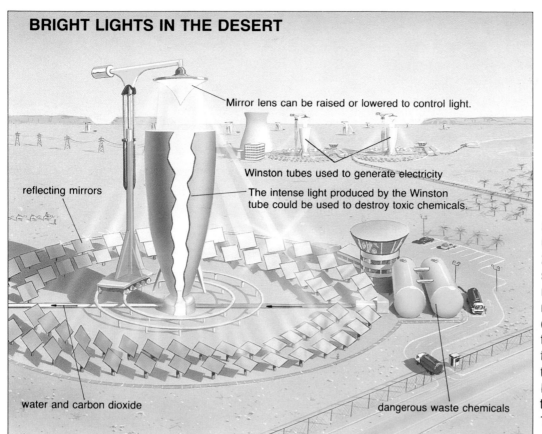

BRIGHT LIGHTS IN THE DESERT

Mirror lens can be raised or lowered to control light.

Winston tubes used to generate electricity

The intense light produced by the Winston tube could be used to destroy toxic chemicals.

reflecting mirrors

water and carbon dioxide

dangerous waste chemicals

Solar power station in California (below). Nearly 2,000 mirrors, each 75 feet square, reflect sunlight onto a receiver on a tower. The mirrors are computer-controlled to follow the path of the sun. Water is pumped through the tower and heated to 937°F (503°C). Steam from the water is used to drive turbines, which produce 10MW for eight hours a day.

Solar power and space power

Sunlight can be converted to electricity directly by using solar cells. Although solar cells are not very efficient—only about one-tenth of the sunlight can be converted to electricity—they will probably improve as new materials are invented. Even now they are useful in sunny countries. For example, in Egypt a main telephone line over 620 miles long is powered entirely by solar cells. This form of power is especially suitable in a desert country such as Egypt, where clear sunlight is available virtually every day. (Night power is supplied by storage batteries charged by solar power during the day.) Solar cells are also used in Egypt and elsewhere to power water pumps, which pump water from irrigation ditches onto the fields.

Solar cells were developed first for the U.S. space program to provide power for satellites and space probes. Space engineers have been examining other ways of taking power directly from space and transferring it down to the Earth's surface. For example, Soviet and French scientists and engineers have a long-term plan to build a huge power station in outer space. This will convert sunlight to microwaves and beam them down to a receiver on Earth, here the microwaves will be converted to electricity. One space power station could produce as much electricity as is now produced from all the power stations of a country the size of the Soviet Union. Even if this project is viable enough for the space

Plant power (above). Will scientists be able to imitate photosynthesis?

power station to be built, it will not take shape until well into the next century. In any case, there are great objections to a potentially dangerous microwave beam several miles wide coming down through the atmosphere.

Plants set the pattern

One of the hopes scientists have for solar power is to try to copy what even the simplest green plant can do in its leaves: trap sunlight and transfer the energy to chemicals directly. There have been many successful attempts to do this in the laboratory, but so far all the methods used would be too expensive to use on a large industrial scale.

The aim is to imitate the first stage of photosynthesis. When sunlight falls on the leaves of plants, the chlorophyll (green chemical) in the leaves uses the sun's energy to split water into the two chemicals it is made of, oxygen and hydrogen. The oxygen is not needed and is released. The energy in the hydrogen is used by the plants to build food. If scientists can develop a cheap way of getting the hydrogen out of water, it could be a fuel to replace oil, coal, and gas. Vehicles

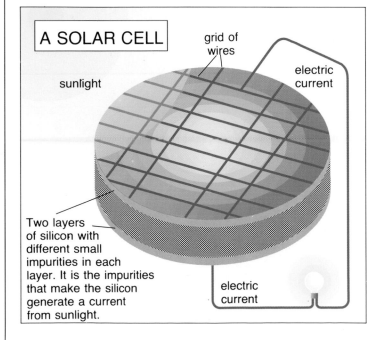

A SOLAR CELL

grid of wires

sunlight

electric current

Two layers of silicon with different small impurities in each layer. It is the impurities that make the silicon generate a current from sunlight.

electric current

could run on it and it could power generators. We would then have a "hydrogen economy," with unlimited fuel from ordinary water.

So far, only one system has come near this process. At Lorrach, in southwest Germany, sunlight reflected by a mirror is directed onto the chemical magnesium hydride (a simple combination of magnesium and hydrogen). When the chemical has reached a temperature of 750°F (400°C), its hydrogen is given off as a gas. The gas is fed to a container holding pure magnesium. The hydrogen combines again with the magnesium and the heat is released. The heat is used to boil water to make steam for electricity generation. The magnesium hydride can be used again and again. The process is over 90 percent efficient.

Telephones tap the power of the sun. Solar-powered telephones like this one in Australia are especially suitable for sunny countries with scattered populations.

Fuel cells and solar cells

When certain chemicals combine to form other chemicals they often generate an electric current. The chemicals can be obtained from simple materials, using solar energy to release them. This system has been used in some plants to produce electricity. The container in which the current is generated is called a fuel cell. One power station in New York operates entirely on fuel cells. Some engineers think the fuel cell will be developed to replace gas in vehicles.

The "Sunraycer," a new automobile from General Motors, is powered by the sun, using solar cells. It was able to cross Australia by a desert route at an average speed of 24 miles per hour. The total energy it used was equivalent to only a few gallons of gas. Although such vehicles could not provide practical, everyday transportation, they do show what proper design can extract from sunlight. As engineers become more skillful at trapping sunlight inexpensively, the likelihood of widespread use of solar energy in the future increases. In the world's middle and lower latitudes, even quite cloudy areas could produce usable solar power fairly cheaply (see map on page 10). The most suitable regions are those with cloudless desert climates. As these are often poor rural regions, solar energy offers many of them the best hope for their future power needs. It could be the most important energy source of all.

See for Yourself
Do this only with an adult present. On a sunny day take a magnifying glass, a length of cotton thread, a clear glass bottle, and a nail. Tie the nail to the thread and suspend it in the bottle. Focus the sun's rays through the glass onto the thread. Hold it steady. What happens?

photosynthesis – the making of food by green plants, using the energy of sunlight.
desalination – the removal of salt from salty water to make it pure (and therefore drinkable).

Green Energy

The most important source of energy comes from the energy trapped by plants from sunlight. Plants such as trees build up their roots, trunks, and branches using this energy. When they are burned the energy is released as heat.

At present about 40 percent of all the energy used in the world comes from burning wood. It is used mainly for domestic cooking and heating. Although wood can be used to power machines, it is not a very suitable fuel for large machines such as electricity generators. The reason for this is that fossil fuels like coal and oil have much greater amounts of energy in them than the same weight of wood: coal contains twice as much energy and oil three times as much. However, unlike coal and oil, wood is a renewable energy source. Each year billions of tons of new fuel are created by green plants. And more than fuel is created, of course. Wood is also used to make paper, chemicals, furniture, and buildings. Because of all the demands for it, wood is becoming scarce in many parts of the world.

Saving trees. Sunderial Bahugowa started a movement to save trees and has persuaded many people in India to protect and replant trees in the Himalayas. Logging has already been stopped in many valleys, so that both fuel and soil have been preserved.

How much wood is left?

As the number of people has increased in the world, more and more forest has been cut down for fuel, buildings, and so on. In many poor parts of the world, wood is now becoming very

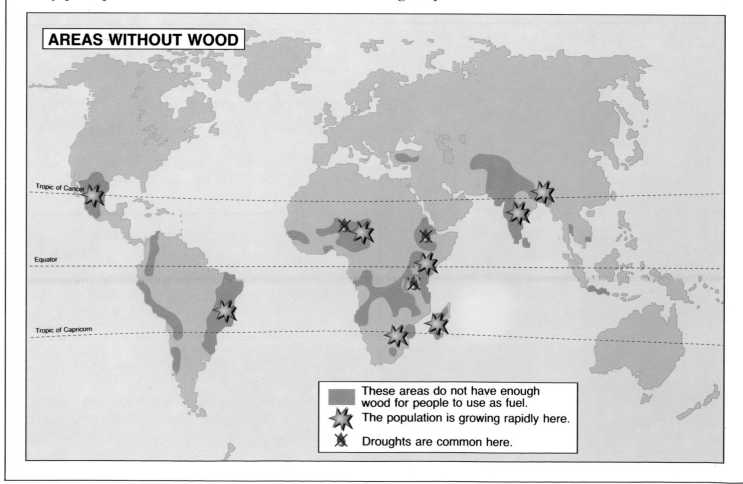

AREAS WITHOUT WOOD

Tropic of Cancer

Equator

Tropic of Capricorn

These areas do not have enough wood for people to use as fuel.

The population is growing rapidly here.

Droughts are common here.

Collecting fuel wood (above) and growing trees (left) in Kenya. In many poor countries it is the women who cook and collect fuel wood for the family. This is why in Kenya it is the women who have taken the lead in replanting trees near their villages.

Forests and pollution

Trees take in carbon dioxide as they grow, so they help to control the amount of carbon dioxide in the air. Cutting and burning large areas of trees, as is happening in the tropical forests, also adds carbon dioxide to the air. If nothing is done to replace trees, the greenhouse effect may happen more quickly. Some power companies have seen this connection between trees and pollution very clearly. In order to soak up the extra carbon dioxide added to the air by a new coal- or oil-burning power station, they plant extra trees in tropical jungles. Power companies in the U.S. did this first and planted trees in Guatemala in Central America. In 1990 a Dutch company planted trees in Indonesia to soak up carbon dioxide from a new power station in Holland. Even though the trees are thousands of miles away from the power stations, the carbon dioxide is taken from the air as a whole.

Seeing connections such as this is part of the science of **ecology.** Ecology is the study of how plants, animals, and people are connected to their environments (living spaces). An ecological view of how we produce our energy is vital if the whole world environment is to be preserved.

scarce (see map on page 16). For example, in Haiti in the Caribbean, nine-tenths of all the trees have been felled for firewood and charcoal (baked wood). Not only is there a fuel shortage in many poor countries, but the land itself is damaged by large-scale tree felling. Trees protect the soil and help to trap water in the ground. Once the trees are removed, the soil may be washed away and the water level may drop. If this happens it may become more difficult to grow food, making the world's poor even poorer.

By the year 2000 about 1 billion people will not have enough wood for their needs. Many countries have started programs to save the forests that remain and to plant new trees. Some of these programs are large-scale ones, organized by governments. Some are on a small scale, organized by the local people (see photographs on this page). But the trees will take a long time to grow big enough to use. There will still be a serious shortage of firewood by the end of the century.

Wood-powered cars

Wood waste, sawdust, shavings, and chips can all be used to produce fuels for vehicles. Two main kinds of fuel are produced at present, but only in small amounts. They are alcohols called methanol and ethanol. Both can also be produced from oil, coal, and gas as well as from plant materials. These two alcohols cause much less pollution than oil-based fuels when they are burned in vehicles.

California will soon introduce strong laws against air pollution, which is a serious problem there. These laws will curtail the use of some oil-based fuels. American, European, and Japanese car makers are trying out new engines which will fit in with these new laws; some are working on battery cars, others on alcohol-based engines. If an alcohol-based engine proves successful, it is likely that methanol will become a major fuel. There will then be a large demand for wood waste as well as straw and other plant remains.

Even sewage waste might eventually be used. In Brazil, the government there has already encouraged the use of sugarcane to produce alcohol for cars, and car makers have produced suitable engines. So by the early twenty-first century the present-day car engine may well be as obsolete as the steam engine.

Smog in Los Angeles. The air is polluted by car exhaust fumes. Cars could run on a gas produced from wood waste (bottom). The gas would not pollute the air.

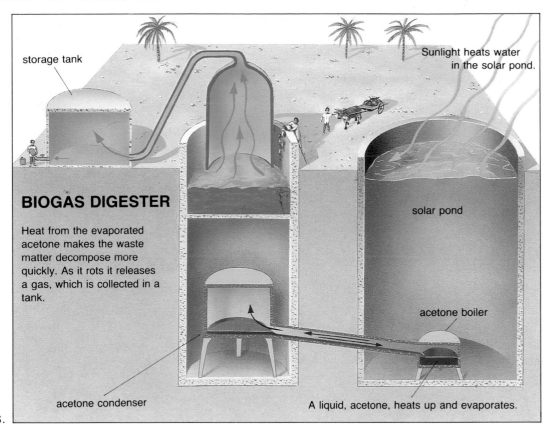

Sugarcane in Brazil (left). The sugarcane is made into an alcohol (ethanol), and used as a fuel for vehicles in Brazil. This is cheaper than importing oil.

storage tank

Sunlight heats water in the solar pond.

BIOGAS DIGESTER

Heat from the evaporated acetone makes the waste matter decompose more quickly. As it rots it releases a gas, which is collected in a tank.

solar pond

acetone boiler

Putting waste to good use. Biogas digesters are being built in India to produce gas for cooking and lighting homes.

acetone condenser

A liquid, acetone, heats up and evaporates.

Energy from garbage

Every day millions of tons of garbage are dumped into holes in the ground and the energy and valuable materials in it are wasted (see page 41). Garbage might soon be recycled (reused) to provide energy.

In Great Britain, the Department of Energy is developing the use of methane gas given off by old, buried garbage. This gas (called landfill gas) begins to generate after the garbage has been underground for about three years. It forms as bacteria attack old food, paper, wood, and other garbage that will rot. In some areas the gas is already being collected and used for central heating, to make electricity, and even to use as fuel to power delivery trucks. Plastic will not decay, but many chemical companies are working to develop plastics that will. When **biodegradable** plastics are produced in quantity they will provide even more methane than garbage. The plastics will not have to be buried, either. Large-scale "digesters" could be set up to draw off the gas from biodegradable plastic waste.

In poor countries small-scale digesters are widely used to decay animal and plant wastes and collect the gas. The gas (called biogas), which is mostly methane, is collected and

used for cooking and lighting homes. Even in some rich countries biogas is now being produced—in Holland for example. Dairy farming in Holland is so intensive, and so many animals are kept in the special dairy sheds, that getting rid of the animal waste has become a great problem. In the past, the waste was spread onto the fields, but the oversupply of waste has completely buried the soil in many places. Therefore many farmers are buying digesters to use the waste to produce biogas. The gas is used for heating and for making electricity with small gas-powered generators. After the biogas has been collected the digested wastes can be compressed and used as valuable fertilizer.

ecology – the science that studies how plants and animals are connected with their environment. Four main aspects are studied: energy (how plants and animals get their food), materials (what they take out of and give to the environment), conditions (climate, soils, and so on), and community (how living things affect each other).
biodegradable – able to be decomposed by bacteria

The Energy of the Wind

Wind power has been used for hundreds of years to blow sailing ships along and to turn windmills. It has been used for electricity production for more than 20 years. The machines that produce the electricity are called **Wind Turbine Generators (WTGs).** A WTG is a form of windmill in which the shaft, turned by the vanes, drives an electric generator. There are still only about 20,000 WTGs in the world, and 15,000 of them are in California. Their total production is only about 2,000 MW. This is the same as the power from one large coal-burning power station. By the year 2000 the electricity production from WTGs is not expected to be much more than 5,000 MW. Why has such an easily obtained energy source not been used more?

The answer is that concentrated fuels like coal, oil, and gas are much cheaper. However, they are only cheap because their production costs do not yet include the costs of repairing the pollution damage they cause. If governments decide that this cost should be part of the price for these fuels, then power from WTGs would be worth buying.

Nuclear power? No thanks!

We know that the possibilities for wind power are very great. Many countries, both rich and poor, have carried out surveys to measure how much wind power they could obtain. Britain could produce as much as 45 TW of wind power. This is equal to the power output from all the nuclear-fueled power stations in the country. In 1989 Britain abandoned all its plans for new nuclear power stations. Figures showed that nuclear power had become too expensive. This was a shock to many people in the power industry in Britain who had always thought that nuclear power was very cheap. The reason it suddenly became expensive was that for the first time the costs of demolishing the older nuclear plants was included in its price. The old plants are extremely dangerous because they contain large quantities of **radioactive** materials. Very expensive special equipment is needed to handle these materials and make sure they do not escape as the plant is being dismantled. Some of the plants are so dangerous they may never be dismantled completely. They will simply be filled with concrete.

These "hidden" costs of nuclear power mean that many countries are likely to pay much more attention in the future to renewable energy sources such as the wind. Surveys have already begun to find the best sites to position lots of WTGs.

Sweden is another country which stopped building nuclear power plants, and the U.S. has built no new nuclear power plants for over 10 years. All these countries are working hard to develop WTGs. However, some other countries like France,

Old sails. Traditional windmills are still used in some parts of the world to grind corn, pump water, and drive machinery.

A wind farm in America. The Altamont Pass in California (inset and main picture) is the site of the biggest wind farm in the world. The winds blowing inland from the sea are funneled through the pass and so increase in speed.

New sails

Club Med One is a wind-assisted French cruise liner. Computers control the trim of the sails, which help to save fuel.

Belgium, Germany, and Japan, which produce lots of electricity by nuclear power (in France it is more than 70 percent) will face great difficulties when the time comes—in about 30 years or so—to dismantle their nuclear stations. If by then they have not developed alternative sources on a large scale, electricity will be expensive and in very short supply. Any new nuclear plants they may build to replace the old ones will produce very expensive electricity, as the price will then have to include the costs of dismantling old plants and disposal of the nuclear wastes.

Designs for the Future

No one yet knows what is the best kind of WTG. Different shapes may suit different locations. Some WTGs have two blades, others have three. Some have bow-shaped blades. One design, from Spain, has no blades at all. It uses a huge area of stretched plastic sheeting. The waves created in the sheeting by the wind are transmitted to pumps.

A WTG in Spain (left).
WTGs in Wales (bottom left).
A WTG in Scotland (center).
WTGs in the U.S (below).

Siting a wind farm

If wind power is to be used effectively, the sites for WTGs must be chosen very carefully to get the best from the local weather conditions. Computers are normally used to analyze information about wind speed, strength, and direction. The choice of site will be combined with the most suitable design of WTG for each particular site. Some sites may need one design, some another (see photographs on this page). There is no doubt that, by 2010, collections of WTGs, known as "wind farms," will be located in all kinds of places and will be a familiar sight.

Joining forces

Since wind does not blow all the time it is a good idea to combine its energy with other sources to try to get as near continuous power production as possible. This has been done on the island of Helgoland in the North Sea, for example. Here solar energy, heat energy from the sea, wind energy, and diesel oil power are combined. Heat is extracted from seawater by a heat pump. The pump takes heat out of the water in the same way as the pump in a freezer takes heat out of the air. The pump is worked by solar-powered electricity, a WTG, or a diesel pump according to the time of day and the weather. The decision to switch from one power type to another is left to a computer which is fed information about the weather from an automatic weather station. The heat from the sea is used to heat houses and to take the salt out of seawater so the islanders have good fresh water.

The Helgoland system has proved to be very efficient. In the future, combined systems like this will become very common because they are cheaper and more reliable than using one kind of alternative power alone. Combined systems are already being installed

Islands in the wind. WTGs may be installed on islands such as the Maldives in the Indian Ocean to produce power for small communities.

along the coast of India and on islands in Indonesia. There are plans to build similar systems in coastal African states such as Senegal and Madagascar. These countries lie in the belts of the Trade Winds, which blow in a strong, predictable direction, so the use of WTGs will save lots of diesel power.

On land or sea?

Some people in Britain have objected to the extensive use of WTGs, saying they will be noisy as they whirl, will spoil the appearance of the countryside, and will take up too much space. These objections have to be taken seriously if the use of wind energy is to be accepted. Most large-scale wind farms will probably be built out at sea, opposite coasts that have shallow enough water to allow building. The first one is planned for the coast of Suffolk. Mountain districts will probably not be used as sites because the hills in Britain produce too much gustiness in the air to be very suitable for wind power generation.

Of course, in countries that are less crowded than those in Europe, these objections will seem much less important. Where the countries are poor as well, the objections will probably hardly be considered at all. By the next century WTGs—either by themselves or as part of combined schemes—will be a familiar part of many landscapes around the world.

---

turbine – a motor with a shaft turned by wind, water, or steam.
WTGs – (Wind Turbine Generators)—turbines turned by the force of the wind to generate electricity.
radioactive – describes any substance that releases high energy radiation.

The Surging Energy of the Sea

Most of the surface of the Earth (about 70 percent) is sea. Five sources of energy have been found in the sea: the waves, the tides, its heat content, the salty water itself, and ocean currents. In various parts of the world people are already supplied with energy from the first four. It is not likely that ocean currents will ever be used, since it would be too expensive to harness their energy.

Riding on the waves

There are two ways to catch the energy of the waves and use it. One way is to build power stations on land, but land-based power stations have one great drawback. They stand at the edge of the sea near rocky cliffs in order to get the maximum power from the waves, so they are in danger from freak waves. The Norwegian wave power station was destroyed by one of these "once in a hundred years" waves in the winter of 1988–89.

Sea power. Water rushes through a narrow rock gully in a wave power device being tested in Scotland (see below).

Gully Wave Generator

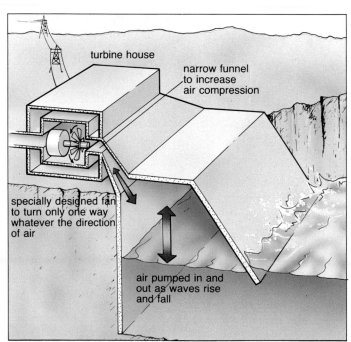

turbine house

narrow funnel to increase air compression

specially designed fan to turn only one way whatever the direction of air

air pumped in and out as waves rise and fall

Wave power in Scotland. Waves are funneled into a rock gully. The constant rise and fall of the water forces air through a turbine which drives a generator. When tests are complete, the device will supply electricity to small, isolated communities.

CLAM—a model for the future? Several wave-energy machines, 14 times bigger than this model, would be linked together in about 100 feet of water, floating and anchored to the sea bed. The crests and troughs of the waves force air into the bags on the side (connected by the blue tubes). As the air pressure builds up it drives turbines housed in the metal cylinder. The electricity is carried ashore by cable.

In spite of this, India intends to build a number of these coastal power stations along harbor breakwaters.

The second way to catch wave energy is by using floating systems tethered in lines. These systems are not so easily damaged by freak waves as they ride up and down on the ocean's surface. They can be set out on long lines and are very efficient. The British **CLAM** system could eventually supply as much electricity as all of the coal-fired power stations do now, and more cheaply. Britain and Japan are both working on such systems. Both countries are especially well placed to extract power from the waves: they both have long coastlines, and many inlets.

Plotting the hot spots

Like wind power, wave power generators cannot just be placed anywhere in the sea. The energy of the waves is affected by the shape of the surface over which they move, in the same way as wind is affected by the land over which it blows. The shape of the seabed distorts the energy pattern of the waves.

Where the bed becomes shallow, it drags on the underside of the wave and reduces its energy. Where the water deepens, the energy of the wave may be concentrated. This is known as an energy "hot spot." Before wave-power machines can be placed, these energy hot spots—which are the best places for the machines—will have to be carefully mapped. Charts of the ocean bottom are matched with studies of the wave patterns over the same area to see where most of the energy is likely to be concentrated.

Many sites around the British coast have already been identified. They are particularly frequent in northwest Scotland, facing the Atlantic, where deep water runs inland into long lochs. However, the prospect of long lines of wave-power machines on a beautiful coast may raise the same objections as for WTGs. Some local fishing grounds might be affected as well. These objections will undoubtedly have to be overcome one way or another as it is very clear that this cheap, abundant, renewable energy source is going to be very important in the future.

Trapping the tide

Where tides are large, huge quantities of water flow in and out of estuaries (river mouths). If a barrier with gates in it is built across a river, the incoming water at high tide can be trapped behind it. As the tide recedes the trapped water can be made to flow back toward the sea past turbines, which turn to generate electricity. A number of these tidal power stations have now been built. France constructed the first on the Rance River in Brittany, and there is one now in Canada on the Bay of Fundy and one in the Soviet Union. There are plans to build a very large plant on the Severn Estuary in Britain (see page 32). However, there are many drawbacks to this use of tidal power.

The first difficulty is cost. Tidal barrages are enormously expensive to build. Many people favor wave power as being much cheaper and simpler than tidal power. A second difficulty is that building a large barrier across an estuary disrupts the marine life—and therefore possibly fisheries. Thirdly, a barrier may limit navigation by ships to ports.

To overcome some of these problems French engineers have designed and built a much less damaging tidal power station than the big dams. This is located on the Brittany coast and uses a very clever system to make the water flow past the turbines. Instead of being held back by dams, the high tide water is trapped in a shallow basin dug out of the rock. As the water recedes toward low tide, water is drawn out of the pool through a tube with a turbine in it. The water turns the turbine as it falls toward the low tide mark. The system works on a principle called siphoning. A number of poor countries in Africa are building versions of this station. Although it can only generate power when the tides are right, it is very cheap.

The heat of the sea

The sea absorbs enormous quantities of heat from the sun in the tropics. This heat is transported around the oceans by warm currents, which take it to cooler latitudes. The cooled water then sinks, or flows back to the warm latitudes as cold currents, on the ocean's surface. The circulation of warm and cold water at the surface is responsible for

much of the Earth's climatic features, as the heat in the sea warms the air above it. It is ocean heat energy that allows people to live in areas like northern Europe and Alaska, where otherwise it would be almost impossible.

The heat energy in the sea is not intense. Nevertheless in the last 20 years scientists and engineers have begun to use its potential for power production, using Ocean Thermal Energy Conversion **(OTEC)** systems. One of the most advanced OTEC systems is in Japan. Here warm surface water is drawn onto land through a pipeline. The heat from the seawater is used to boil a liquid that has a much lower boiling point than water. The gas produced is then used instead of normal steam to turn electricity generator turbines. The gas is then condensed back to a liquid again by cooling it with cold seawater piped from lower levels of the ocean. Such programs provide a cheap way to generate electricity in tropical lands with very warm seas.

Trapping the tide in Brittany, France (left). Notice that the water on the righthand side of this tidal barrage (dam)—built across the Rance estuary—is higher than on the lefthand side. The water flows through turbines below the dam. A lock between the building and the parking lot allows ships to pass through the dam.

When fresh water meets salt water. Any country with a coastline broken by rivers could use the Japanese osmosis system to generate cheap electricity (see below).

Saltwater energy

Fresh water has more energy than salt water. So, if fresh and salt water are brought next to each other but separated by a very fine membrane (sheet), water will seep from the fresh water to the salt water. This flow from high energy liquid to a lower energy liquid through a membrane is called **osmosis**. Japanese engineers have invented a new kind of membrane to keep fresh river and salty sea water apart. The pressure builds up on the salty side and can be used to drive machinery, including electricity generators. This is probably one of the simplest forms of power production ever devised. It is also a true imitation of nature. Trees move water through their trunks for many feet without any energy cost to themselves by means of osmosis. The Japanese imitation of this process is one of the most efficient forms of power generation so far. Over 90 percent of the energy is useable. Such power plants may become widespread.

See for Yourself
● Cut a dandelion stalk into strips lengthways. Put the strips into a saucer with a little tap water. You will see the rapid osmosis of water into the dandelion stalk. Now stir about three teaspoons of sugar into the water in the saucer. Water will slowly move out from the stalk into the more concentrated sugar water.

CLAM – the name given to a British wave pressure system.
OTEC – Ocean Thermal Energy Conversion: systems which extract heat from seawater.
osmosis – the movement of a liquid from one solution to another through a membrane (thin sheet). The flow is always from the weaker to the stronger solution.

The Energy of Falling Water

Water that flows downhill to the sea does so under the pull of gravity. Water that is uphill has **potential gravitational energy,** because it can be made to move downhill if a channel is available. If the water is led over a waterwheel as it flows downhill it can turn the wheel. In 1881 a waterwheel was used to produce electricity for the first time by powering a turbine to light a large country house in Northumberland, England. Today this form of power is named **hydroelectric power,** or HEP.

Unlike coal, oil, or nuclear fuel it is a true renewable power source. It is also very efficient. Ninety percent of the energy of falling water can be turned to electric power.

Flooding the land

Huge dams are needed to produce HEP on a large scale. Some large plants are high in the mountains, like those in the Rockies in the U.S. or the Alps in Europe. These plants rely on a small volume of water falling fast from a great height to power the turbines. Other dams, like those on the rivers of the Russian plain, the lower Rhône valley in France, or the Amazon in South America, rely on large volumes of water falling a short way to give the power. Both kinds of dam are expensive to build. If poor countries want big dams they have to borrow large amounts of money to build them.

In some countries dam-building may flood so much land that many people have to move

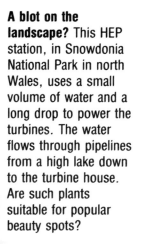

A blot on the landscape? This HEP station, in Snowdonia National Park in north Wales, uses a small volume of water and a long drop to power the turbines. The water flows through pipelines from a high lake down to the turbine house. Are such plants suitable for popular beauty spots?

to new land on which to farm. Many Indians are protesting against the government's plans to build a huge series of hydroelectric dams in the central part of India. As many as two million people will lose their homes. Similar problems may arise in China, which has plans to more than double the output of HEP, even though it will lose valuable land under the lakes formed behind the dams.

Fever and fish

Loss of land is not the only difficulty caused by the lakes behind large dams. Dams in tropical countries may provide breeding areas for disease-carrying insects. Near large dams like the Volta plant in Ghana, West Africa, and the Aswan Dam in Egypt, outbreaks of the deadly "rift valley fever" have occurred. Before the dams were created the fever was unknown in both these areas.

Fish and other creatures that live in rivers may also be affected by large dams. Because the water behind the dams is nearly stagnant, the deep water gradually loses its oxygen. The water which passes through the turbines or is released from the dam base downriver is unsuitable for normal aquatic life, so the rivers have lost much of their fish.

Waterwheels at a standstill in the Pennine Hills, England (left). These waterwheels once drove machinery in the mine nearby. For centuries water and wind provided the main energy sources for industry before fossil fuels were used.

Inside a hydroelectric generator house at a dam in the Soviet Union. (Inset) Water is released at the Aswan High Dam in Egypt after passing through the turbines.

Silting up

Further problems can occur with silting up of the dams. One of the most spectacular examples of this is the Aswan High Dam in Egypt. Here the Nile River is liable to seasonal flooding, which carries with it lots of mud and sand. The mud and sand accumulate behind the dam and will probably eventually stop its operation as a power source. It is interesting to note that before the dam was built there were many warnings by scientists that the dam would silt up. These warnings were ignored, even though the farmers of the river valley farther downstream relied on the floods to spread new silt on their land every year. The silt acted as a fertilizer. Now the farmers have to buy artificial fertilizers.

Calling a halt

A much more cautious approach to the building of dams is needed in the future, and possible ecological effects must be taken into account before a site is approved. In northern Quebec, Canada, a huge plan to build dams on the rivers flowing into James Bay on Hudson Bay has been postponed. Many people objected to the effects the plan would have on what is an almost untouched forest wilderness. The area would be spoiled, not only by the dams, but also by the roads and quarries needed to build the dams. In Brazil, plans which would have flooded thousands of square miles of the Amazon River basin have also been abandoned as people have become aware of the role the Amazon forest plays in soaking up carbon dioxide from the air.

There are other signs that the approach to dam building is much more cautious than it used to be. A major plant in Venezuela on the Caroni River has been built in stages. Any problems can therefore be solved before the next stage is built, and the amount of electricity produced is limited to what is needed by the country at the time. The first stage was begun in 1963 to produce 1,823 MW. The dam has been raised twice since then to increase its production to nearly 3,000 MW. There are plans to raise it yet again to

Waterfalls in Sri Lanka. This small hydroelectric plant produces 10 kw of electricity, enough for the local village.

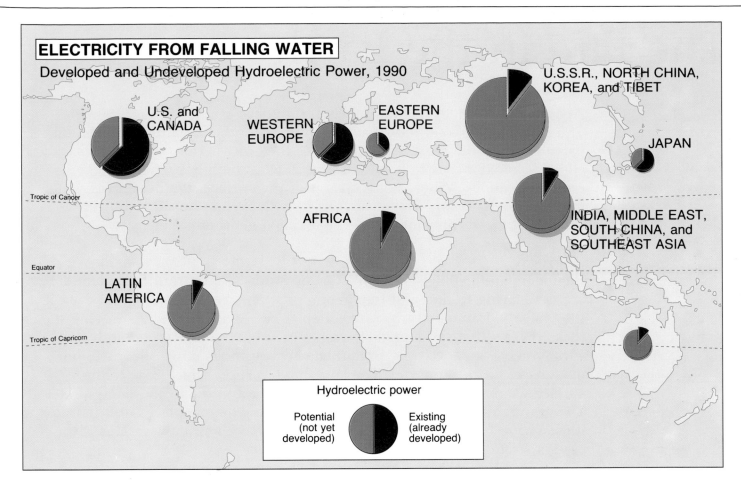

ELECTRICITY FROM FALLING WATER
Developed and Undeveloped Hydroelectric Power, 1990

U.S. and CANADA

WESTERN EUROPE

EASTERN EUROPE

U.S.S.R., NORTH CHINA, KOREA, and TIBET

JAPAN

Tropic of Cancer

AFRICA

INDIA, MIDDLE EAST, SOUTH CHINA, and SOUTHEAST ASIA

Equator

LATIN AMERICA

Tropic of Capricorn

Hydroelectric power

Potential (not yet developed)

Existing (already developed)

take its production to nearly 20,000 MW. This will make it the world's largest single hydroelectric plant. Other new plants are following this pattern of cautious growth.

Small is beautiful
The development of large HEP plants in Africa, South America, and Asia (see map on this page) may be very slow, because of the cost. However, in recent years new kinds of small-scale plants have been set up very successfully. In Southeast Asia there is abundant water most of the year. Many of the hillsides are steep, with many waterfalls. A number of small-scale plants are being built, often by Swedish, German, and other European firms. A typical plant might use a fall of water of only a few feet and produce only 200 kilowatts. This might seem very small when compared with the many megawatts of a major hydroelectric dam, but to a village which has no electric power it is a great help. Even in Britain small plants are being developed. They will produce as little as 5 MW of power and serve mainly local needs in villages and small towns.

The future for HEP
In spite of all the difficulties, HEP offers some important advantages. It produces no greenhouse gases, it is renewable, it is very efficient, and there are huge reserves available. The potential world production is about 36,000 TW. This is about the figure for all the world's electricity produced at present. Only some of this potential power will ever be harnessed, because of the difficulties described. Nevertheless, by 2020 HEP will be supplying about one-fifth of all the world's electricity. The benefits to our polluted atmosphere will be enormous.

potential gravitational energy – the energy of any material at a higher level than another material, for example water in a dam above a power station. This energy is converted to kinetic energy when it is released and allowed to fall or run downhill under the pull of gravity.
hydroelectric power – electricity generated by turbines turned by the force of falling water.

The Fire in the Earth

About 15 to 20 miles below your feet, the rocks are hot enough to melt. The thin shell of solid rock that allows us and other creatures to exist on Earth is called the **crust**. In some places the crust is thin and it cracks, allowing molten rock to flow out. This is what happens when lava spills out of volcanoes. Where hot rock is near the surface, the heat turns water in the rocks to steam. The steam can be collected and used to power steam turbines. This kind of energy is called **geothermal energy.**

Hot rocks

Engineers and geologists (scientists who study rocks) around the world are now trying to find and trap geothermal energy. Not all places, even if they have volcanoes nearby, are suitable. However, carefully studying the rocks reveals that some unlikely places may have rocks hot enough to supply geothermal energy. Britain has no volcanoes now, of course, but millions of years ago it did. The lava (molten rock) which rose to the surface was trapped in the crust. This solidified into a rock called granite. The granite may be completely buried still, as in some places in Britain, or it may have been uncovered as rocks above have worn away. This is the case in southwest Britain.

The granite is made of materials which contain chemicals that give off heat. They do this because they are radioactive (see page 23). The heat is trapped in the rock underground and gradually the rocks have become hotter and hotter. In Britain the rock two miles below the surface has

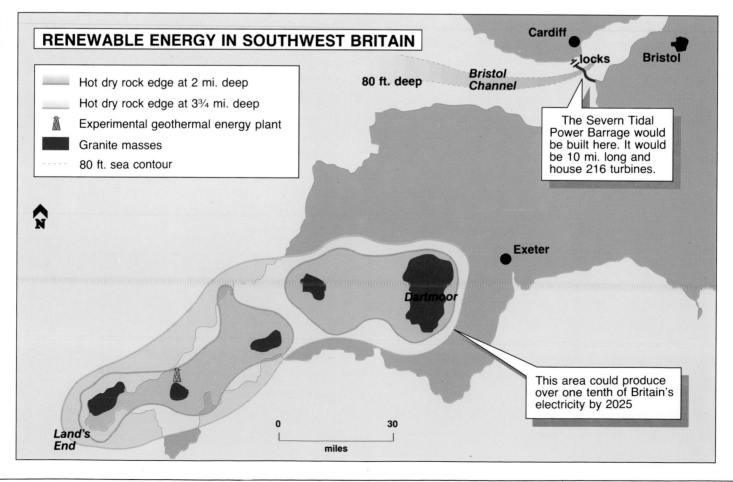

RENEWABLE ENERGY IN SOUTHWEST BRITAIN

Hot dry rock edge at 2 mi. deep
Hot dry rock edge at 3¾ mi. deep
Experimental geothermal energy plant
Granite masses
80 ft. sea contour

Cardiff
locks
Bristol
80 ft. deep
Bristol Channel

The Severn Tidal Power Barrage would be built here. It would be 10 mi. long and house 216 turbines.

Exeter

Dartmoor

This area could produce over one tenth of Britain's electricity by 2025

N

Land's End

0   30
miles

reached about 400°F (200°C). The heat can be used by pumping water down to this depth and letting it circulate through cracks in the hot, dry rocks. The water turns to steam and rises up a borehole, where it can be used to power turbines. If the holes were made deeper, down to four miles so that even hotter rocks were tapped, Britain could use this energy source to provide one-fifth of the country's future electricity needs. However, it has one drawback: it is not a truly renewable energy source. The heat in the rocks took millions of years to build up. Once the heat is used, the energy could not be replaced (except over millions of years, of course). Nevertheless, it is still worth developing, since it will last over 100 years before the rock becomes too cool to use.

Granites like those in southwest Britain occur in many parts of the world, often in poor countries. This source of power could become important in the next 30 years as more hot, dry rocks are discovered. One way to find the reserves quickly is to look for them from outer space by satellites. Remote sensing detects where extra heat is being released to the surface from underground heat reservoirs.

Anglo-French Links

Paris   English Channel   Southampton

Some very unlikely geothermal sources have already been discovered by accident in the process of drilling for other energy sources, such as oil. In southern England and northern France a huge reservoir of hot water has been found soaking a bed of rock named the Old Red Sandstone. The water temperature is about 167°F (76°C). This is hot enough to be used for heating buildings. In Southampton and in towns in northern France it is beginning to be used in this way. In Paris alone there are now over 40 different heating systems using this hot water. Like the heat in the British granite it is not truly a renewable resource. However, it is likely to last for many decades and there are a large number of towns where it is sufficiently near the surface for its use to become even more common.

Tapping volcanic heat

Truly renewable geothermal energy needs active or recently active volcanoes as sources of heat. Many countries around the world that lie near active volcanic regions now tap this resource for heating and power production. They include the U.S., New Zealand, Mexico, Italy, Japan, and Iceland. Iceland has so much potential geothermal power from its volcanic sources that plans exist to export the electricity it generates to Scotland by submarine cable. In fact, if Britain was to invest in Icelandic geothermal electricity production, this source could supply over 10 percent of the country's electricity needs. This source of electricity would be cheaper than that of most hydroelectric systems.

To produce even more power than geothermal energy alone, some plans combine geothermal with other energy sources. For example, in northern California hot water from the Wendel Hot Springs is pumped from wells 6,500 feet deep. The water temperature is at 482°F (250°C). This hot water is added to water heated by waste from the local forestry industry. The plant can generate 39 MW of electricity cheaply.

Superheat in Iceland. Iceland is an island on a huge crack in the Earth's crust. Lava lies very near the surface and water in the ground is heated beyond the boiling point by the lava. Steam from the hot water is used to drive turbines.

Energy for the future (right)? This beautiful landscape in the Pennine Hills, England, could be developed as a geothermal power site. Rocks underground are hot enough to heat water to steam, which would drive turbines.

Swimming in hot water in Iceland. When the water from underground has been used at the power station, it is still very hot. It is fed into the Blue Lagoon, where people can swim in comfort, even in winter.

There are some dangers in using geothermal energy, however. For example, if too much water is extracted from the rocks or too much water is pumped into dry rocks, the underground pressure conditions may change and the rock could start to slip along any weak cracks. In Texas and southwestern parts of the U.S. the removal of groundwater has caused small earthquakes. Most geothermal plants nowadays have to be carefully planned and the deep rocks surveyed in detail.

Nobody knows how much power we may eventually be able to generate from geothermal energy. If the example of Britain, where there are no nearby volcanoes, is repeated in many other places the possibilities are enormous. In places where there are volcanoes either active now or active in the recent past the possibilities are even greater. As many of these regions, for example South and Central America, Central Africa, and Southeast Asia are regions with poor countries, this may be one of the great hopes for increasing those regions' wealth. Even in Europe, the possibilities have hardly been touched. In central France, for example, there are many extinct volcanoes and even hot springs. Developing this resource might be more sensible than the huge nuclear program that France has decided on.

crust – the thin shell of solid rock of the planet. Its depth varies between 15 to 20 miles. It is made of crystalline rocks like granite and a dark crystalline rock called basalt. Its outer part is often made of solidified sands, mud, and lime (sediments). These outer rocks contain the fossil fuels.

geothermal energy – heat energy from water heated to steam by hot rocks below the surface. Where the steam is under pressure from the rocks superheated steam is created. Here the boiling point of water is raised by pressure to above 210°F (100°C).

The Fifth Fuel: Conservation

Engineers and energy scientists say that energy conservation (saving energy) is the fifth fuel after coal, oil, gas, and uranium. By this they mean that every unit of energy saved is a unit of energy they do not have to generate by burning.

Saving energy—and money

One of the biggest energy conservation programs in the world is that of the Bonneville Power Administration in Utah. It began in 1984 and by 1987 had saved 690 million dollars in fuel costs. Over the five years to 1989 the energy saved was 220 MW (equal to one small coal-fired power station). By 2010 the program will have saved 2,750 MW. This is equal to the output of four medium-sized nuclear power stations. These savings have proved to the United States government and industrialists that saving energy is good business. It is also the quickest route to reducing pollution.

In Britain it is known that every pound spent on conserving electricity in the average three-bedroom house would reduce electricity consumption by 38 kw and carbon dioxide release by 92 lbs. a year. Of course, it would also reduce the electricity bill, so that the money spent would be recovered after two years. In the country as a whole, energy saving in homes could reduce the amount of coal burned by 45 million

Houses in the wall. A housing program in Newcastle, England, saves energy in several ways. High-rise apartments are built into a mile-long wall (white in the picture) which faces south. The wall reflects sunlight, and keeps the wind off the low-rise houses built on the south side. The apartments and houses are well-insulated, and many of the houses are heated by water from a plant that burns the city's garbage. The elevated railroad cuts the amount of traffic in the city.

tons per year. Even quite simple changes like switching to a more efficient and longer-lasting lightbulb could remove the need to build extra power stations.

In spite of the obvious advantages of energy conservation, most industrialized countries have only just begun to take it seriously. Many individuals have incorporated energy-saving devices into their homes, but it was only in 1990 that the British government, for example, began to give serious emphasis to energy conservation. This followed the realization that continuing to produce more electricity by building nuclear power stations was not going to be possible.

Heat from the sun. Solar panels provide a least 25 percent of the heat required by this house in Ohio throughout the year. The panels would provide more heat in a climate where sunshine is more constant.

Energy efficiency at work in Holland (below). The unusual shape of the NMB Bank Building in Amsterdam helps to keep out traffic noise. The walls, floors, and windows are insulated with new materials, and solar panels warm the air inside. Rainwater is collected to humidify the air and to water the indoor plants.

The greenhouse effect? A south-facing sun room traps the sunlight and provides warm air for the whole house. In another house, large windows on the south side (inset bottom) let in warmth while smaller windows on the north side (inset top) keep out the cold.

Where to save power

In developed countries the two main users of energy are buildings and vehicles. In the United States, for example, 37 percent of all the energy used is consumed in buildings of all types, mostly for heat and light. Machines use relatively little energy. Cars and other vehicles consume about 27 percent of all the rest of the energy used. In poor countries relatively little energy is used in buildings for heating and lighting as the climates are often warm enough for natural heating and there are few large buildings. The bulk of the energy used is for cooking and for vehicles. So conservation programs must concentrate on these areas.

In a new light. New fluorescent lights (below) use one-fifth of the energy needed by filament lightbulbs, which most people use, and they last eight times as long.

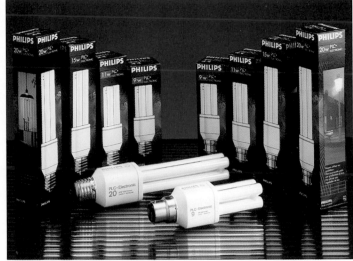

Keeping warm. A new stove hood (top left) takes warm air from the kitchen and uses the heat to warm fresh air to help heat the rest of the house. Solar panels (left and on title page) can be used to heat water. Storm windows (bottom left) and insulation in the walls and roof (below) help to keep houses warm and save on fuel bills.

Saving energy in buildings

Most of the energy used in homes can be saved in fairly simple, cheap ways. Better insulation and control of drafts are the two main ways in older buildings. In new buildings, insulation can be built into the design at the start. In the U.S. some power companies employ staff to check for poor insulation in customers' homes. They offer the homeowner free insulation and energy-saving advice. The cost is included in all customers' bills. As the companies say, "Every kilowatt saved is a kilowatt we don't have to generate." In Britain and West Germany the governments offer grants to homeowners to encourage them to improve their insulation. Other developed countries have similar programs.

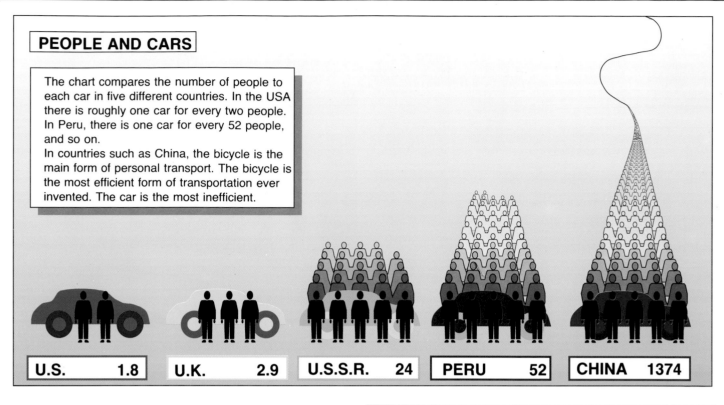

PEOPLE AND CARS

The chart compares the number of people to each car in five different countries. In the USA there is roughly one car for every two people. In Peru, there is one car for every 52 people, and so on.

In countries such as China, the bicycle is the main form of personal transport. The bicycle is the most efficient form of transportation ever invented. The car is the most inefficient.

| U.S. | 1.8 | U.K. | 2.9 | U.S.S.R. | 24 | PERU | 52 | CHINA | 1374 |

Saving fuel in vehicles

Every day about 100,000 cars are built in the world. Over 80,000 of them are bought in developed countries. Imagine what it would be like if, in 100 years' time, cars were owned by all the people of the world at the same rate that they are owned in the U.S. now. This would mean at least 5 billion cars in the world. If the cars used fuel at the same rate, too, they would burn over one trillion gallons

Testing (above). This American experimental car runs on electricity. It has a range of about 150 miles (240 kms) before it needs recharging, but the range will increase as battery design improves.

Charging up. This electric car is recharging its batteries at a public electrical outlet in California.

of fuel per year. The world would either quickly run out of fuel or the atmosphere would become completely polluted.

It seems clear that the future of the car as we know it is limited. People may still have personal transportation, and it may still be called a car, but the vehicles will be very different from ours. They will be light, energy-efficient, nonpolluting, and probably not made of steel, which is too heavy and takes lots of energy to make. The kinds of cars we have now—heavy, fast, dangerous, noisy, and polluting—will be found only in museums and our descendants will wonder why we allowed such monsters on our roads.

The best way to save energy in vehicles would be to redesign the car for efficiency and not speed. New engines that use less-polluting fuels such as alcohol, diesel, electricity, and even solar power (see page 15) are already being developed. New body materials such as fiberglass and other plastics are being used. However, the most effective way to save fuel immediately would be to reduce driving speeds. The U.S. has already shown how much fuel can be saved by restricting maximum speeds to 55 or 65 mph. The lower speeds have also reduced the incidence of accidents as well as saving energy. Will other countries reduce their speed limits in view of the enormous benefits?

Recycling

In 1989 the city of Sheffield in England decided to see how much of its garbage could be recycled. The city produces about 250,000 tons of solid waste material a year. The aim is to recycle half of this by 1993. If the program pays for itself or makes a profit, many other places are likely to follow suit. In Britain as a whole the cost of simply collecting and dumping garbage is about 1.2 billion dollars a year. If the useful energy and materials could be extracted from this garbage and sold, it would generate about 1.3 billion dollars. So the recycling would actually be profitable. If special arrangements were made to use the heat from burning the nonusable materials, the profit would be even greater. In Germany for instance, whole districts are now heated by water warmed by the burning of town garbage.

Of course it is not only garbage that can be recycled. For over 100 years wool has been recycled in the mills of West Yorkshire, England. Metals such as aluminum, steel, copper, zinc, and lead, which require expensive energy in their production, are constantly recycled. Glass and paper are now recycled, too. In Holland about 60 percent of glass is now recycled.

Unfortunately, sudden increases in recycled materials can spoil the market for selling it.

Saving scrap metal.
Recycling steel and other materials saves energy and has become a big business in developed countries. In the U.S. more than 20,000 cars are scrapped each day.

When West Germany introduced laws to make people recycle their waste paper, so much paper was collected that the price for the recycled material fell drastically. In the future, if recycling is to be important as a way of conserving energy and materials, it will have to be planned more carefully. Experiments like those in Sheffield and other western cities will produce the essential information for making recycling efficient.

Garbage for heat. Waste materials can be burned to give heat for buildings.

Storing energy

In some hydroelectric plants, energy can be stored as potential gravitational energy (see page 28), by using surplus power to pump water back up to a lake at a higher level. The water can be allowed to run down through the power station again when demand is high. A similar idea is used in the Hamburg area of West Germany, except that here it is compressed air which is stored. The air is pumped into an underground chamber, using surplus power. The air is forced in just as air is forced into a bicycle tire. When demand is high the air is released to power air-driven turbines. There are many places where similar systems could be used. Hollows underground in old salt mines, or even natural caves in limestone could be used. About one-third of the great central plains of the U.S. has suitable structures underground. Many of the structures are old oil wells into which air could be pumped.

When half-time is called during the British Cup final soccer matches in England and Scotland each year, all over the country millions of electric kettles are switched on to make tea. The sudden load on the electricity grid is one of the greatest it has to bear in the whole year. By the time people are back at their television sets the power generated to meet the extra demand is only just reaching its peak. Much of this extra power is then wasted. As yet, electric power cannot be stored directly. If there was a supply of stored electricity on hand, the power stations could work at their most efficient levels all the time.

In the 1980s direct storage of electricity became a possibility. New materials were discovered called superconductors. Superconductors are special mixtures of chemicals that have no resistance to electric current. That is, they produce no heat when electricity passes through them. If cables of this material carried electricity there would be no loss of power. (About five percent of all electric power is lost by the resistance of the cables used now.)

Superconductors are only one example of the many new materials that will be developed as the next century approaches. Many of these will undoubtedly make the task of conserving energy much easier. Therefore, they will also make the task of conserving the planet much easier.

Conclusion: Less Is More

A small clearing in the rain forest, New Guinea.

Clearings for roads and oil rigs in the rain forest, Brazil.
These pictures provide another example of "less is more." People from industrial countries often cut down large areas of forest—without replanting—for mining, cattle ranches, roads, factories, and so on. The native people who live in the forest, on the other hand, make only small clearings to grow their food. They move on after a few years to new clearings so the forest can grow again. Less destruction means more resources for everyone.

One of the first lessons engineers learn when they design a machine is that less is more: to be efficient, a machine must give more work for less energy.

We can see examples of greater efficiency all around us. Cars, televisions, radios, and computers are already lighter and use less energy than those built only a few years ago. In the U.S. the idea of energy efficiency is seen as especially important. Machines have to be labeled with their energy efficiency rating. Thus people can compare for themselves how expensive appliances will be to run if they buy them. This kind of labeling will be required in most countries soon. Neither individuals nor the world as a whole can afford inefficient machines.

One of the greatest enemies to efficiency in machines, whether they are producing power or using it, is friction. Engineers see it as the main enemy to efficient design. Friction is the production of heat caused by one part rubbing against another. One of the great hopes for the future is that new materials with very low friction ratings will become cheap enough to replace the metal bearings lubricated by grease and oil we have now. Low-friction bearings

would save enormous amounts of energy. A friction-free car could halve its fuel consumption immediately. If all machinery, industrial and domestic, used bearings of the new material, the demand for power would fall dramatically. Suitable materials already exist—they were developed for use in the U.S. space program—but they are still very expensive. They can only be used at present for very special needs like artificial hip joints. However, in the U.S., Europe, and Japan, car manufacturers are developing low-friction engines based on similar materials.

You have seen in this book that there is no shortage of ideas for how to get our energy supplies in the future. By the middle of your lifetime, what we now call alternative energy supplies will be quite normal. Our present "normal" ways will then have become the alternatives nobody wants.

Glossary

biogas – the gas, mostly methane, given off by plant and animal waste as it is decomposed by bacteria in a "digester."

desalination – the removal of salt from salty water.

ecology – the study of the relationships between people, plants, and animals and their environment.

energy – something that is capable of making things work.

environment – the surroundings in which people, plants, and animals live.

fossil fuels – coal, oil, and natural gas, derived from plant and animal remains trapped in rocks.

geothermal energy – heat energy derived from steam heated by hot rocks in the Earth's crust.

gravity – a force of attraction that, on Earth, pulls liquids and solids to the ground.

greenhouse gases – gases such as carbon dioxide that trap heat in the atmosphere.

hydroelectric power – electricity generated by turbines turned by the force of falling water.

membrane – thin sheet of material.

methane – a gas given off by plant and animal waste as it rots. Also called natural gas and marsh gas.

methanol – an alcohol made from wood, which can be used as a fuel for vehicles and which gives off less pollution than fossil fuels.

oil – a complex mixture of chemicals, all of them having carbon, hydrogen, and oxygen as a basis. Oil can be made into different fuels, plastics, and artificial fibers such as nylon.

osmosis – the movement of a weak liquid to a stronger liquid through a membrane (thin sheet).

OTEC – Ocean Thermal Energy Conversion. The system extracts heat from seawater.

photosynthesis – the making of food by green plants, using the energy of sunlight.

potential gravitational energy – the energy of any material which is at a higher location than another material.

renewable energy – energy that cannot be used up, no matter how much is used. Coal, oil, and mined gas are not renewable. Once their energy is released it cannot be renewed. The sun, wind, and sea are the main sources of usable renewable power.

solar cell – a device made of silicon that can convert light to electric current.

solar energy – the different kinds of energy radiated by the sun. The wavelengths of radiation range from short, high-energy types to long, low-energy types.

turbine – a shaft turned by wind, water, gas, or steam. The shaft may be attached to machinery to produce mechanical power or to an electric generator to produce electric current.

WTG – a wind turbine generator, in which the turbine is turned by the wind to generate electricity.

Further Reading

Conway, Lorraine *Energy* (Superific Science Series) Good Apple 1985

Cross, Mike *Wind Power* Watts 1985

Dineen, Jacqueline *Energy from Sun, Wind, and Tide* (World's Harvest Series) Enslow 1988

Middleton, N. *Atlas of World Issues* Oxford 1988

Energy Raintree Publishers Inc. Staff (Science and Its Secrets Series) Raintree 1988

Yates, Madeleine *Sun Power: The Story of Solar Energy* Abingdon 1982

Index

First published in England, 1990,
by Evans Brothers Ltd., London